waterways books

Passages of Time

waterways.

releasing new voices, revealing new perspectives

Passages of Time

waterways
www.waterways-publishing.com
an imprint of flipped eye publishing

First Edition
Copyright © James Byrne, 2002
Reprinted 2002, 2004, 2006, 2009
Cover Image © Kitty Sullivan, 2006
Cover Design © flipped eye publishing, 2006

ISBN-10: 0-9542247-2-8
ISBN-13: 978-0-9542247-2-1

Printed and Bound in the United Kingdom

'All sound is nothing but silence being moved'
- Tony Buzan

Passages of Time

James Byrne
2002

Thank you to Rosie Levine for reading the early junk, to my family for letting me use their fingerprints, to anyone at The Poetry Café, Covent Garden, especially John Citizen, Valeria & Victoria Mosley and, lastly, a huge debt of gratitude to Nii Parkes for believing the words.

J.B.
July 2002

Passages of Time

Ends or Destinations

The Myth of Silence

There is never an end to it
The ceaseless wailing, the slap
Of wind on willow fingertips

Or the language of shipwrecks
Rocks and hollow daylight, waves
In conversation with the harbours edge

Or the symphonic quiver of fish
With barcode fins, doe-eyed, nomadic
A mile or so from land

There is never an end to it
The voiceless calling, the ghosts
Of merchantmen, adrift at sea

Or the lovers they left behind, whispering
Sweet nothings, poised to confess dread
Through a salted tide

There is never an end to it
The poets voyage, seeking to slur the taste
Of a new word

Never an end to it, the footprints
Of history once made
Upon the white fruit of a moon.

Economy

The amber hour has run its course
Skirted whisky across the fading city
Made beautiful innumerable ashen walls
Pasted its shade on tower-block sills

Now, slowly jamming forever homeward
The shrill of traffic scrolls pen-mapped streets
A sound so fierce our ears jewel to it
Until the argument reaches our skulls

We sit with our capes and unmerited visions
Well-mannered skeletons marked by reticence
Delineating the day, its endless twitches and sirens
Its time-honoured cures and heartbreaks

Old busy-body to the left crackles
Local woman she says, fountain chatterer, I say
Her thoughts silences held by a mesh of wires
Her memories spray-blown and shop-worn

Anguished yet restlessly mobile I exit
Walk down the road that has become home
The same road that keeps inviting me back
Thudding the letterbox with debt duties

Walk down the road that has become home
Head full of cutouts and loves irretrievables
Forgetting, I look up and catch the enormity
A pack of stars in full cry icing the heavens.

The Sea Stones

For what do they endure?
Oceans eddy and lap the silent shore
Wave-crash! Transparent tongues puncture the night sky
Raw pulse basses the dark like a dead self-singing
Delirium! What purpose does it hold? The ongoing
Cat yawn of an incestuous river whitening in the half-light

How quickly the sea forgets its voices
Its endless ledges and sirens as if a brief act of pride
Or something else buried irretrievably deep
The handprint of starfish on shipwreck
So human though our hands tend elsewhere
Upstream on the verge of flame or breath
Enduring their own hour, almost ocean-less
But for the faint wisp of salt leaking like dream

But let us remember the sea
How quickly it forgets its creations
Its fishbone secrets its pebbles hopelessly lost for location
Sleepless nets docking tide-pulse from dawn to dusk
Scent of a gull kissing silted-lips before western migration
The watery transition of soul to bone and then bone to dust
Age-old rocks assemble on the shore like a peaceable battalion
Shell-swirls echo time time-past from a long since parted generation
Returned like fibres of memory, sleep-threaded, innocuous

At what cost this endurance?
Brittle air-streams shift north like a ghost possessed
Violent sobs resound over the courtyard heath
As if made by bird-squall unfurled in a tree
And nature's unwritten sonnets crackle in a fern bed
Deathless in the wind's army of teeth

And so the continuum, inland
An ageless sun mollifies diagonal javelins of rain
Light bobs and feathers fingernails of oak
Redwoods and rose-bloom succumb to deep hypnosis
Listening in like a lapsed odour of God
Until the strange renewal of self in motion

I have come so far
The sea washed me up once, though the sun fires my heart
With a voice that the dead make from their silence

And today, today I stand on the shore caught up
In a language that sea stones use when talking back at me
Sea gulls circle the air, but they must be deaf,
Why else would they endlessly twitter?
But the stones, the sea-stones, what are they speaking of?

Slick

The ships were long rollers

Limitless, undefined by foam-padded silence
Sleeked lean, sea-burnt from unending wave-crash

On the drowned curtain of an earth-old pulse
Drifting towards Canada's eye-white shoulder-blade
Through horizons brow, tipped with gold.

The buoys had been raised well
Positioned to marker the lacquered fog
That swept in from Michigan's coiled hipbone

They bobbed like dance-floor onlookers
Disciplined by merging levels of arrhythmic salt

I was there too, innocuous, in the undertow
Marvelling at the onomatopoetics of sea
Repeating it in the nativity half-light, sea, sea, sea!

The ships were long rollers striding on ancient fires,
From one oil slicked as if from a wound
Curdling ripple-cracks with waif-like excrement

Faintly, in the distance
A collar of barcode-fanned fish cried out
Sea, sea, sea!

Overhead, a solitary gull flew
Shadowing the sky, God-like

Head-bowed down
By the permanence of flight

It trailed off into dusk
To become legend or prayer

Driving Ohio

The land is measured out
In rows of brick and corn

Infinite air-streams cascade
Over the scarlet earth

Whole gusts grapple and mix
In pools of shimmering heat

Occasionally a church cancels the lawn
And a musty plume

Tricks the bleak pottery
Of my nose

Offerings of crucifix bleed through stone
Wife-less and still in the honey-vined silence

Yet I am somewhere else
Thinking of how God's splintered hands
Could have been painted by Michelangelo

And then it hits me;
Out here in the furnace of Ohio
Everything a distance away from being unseen

I keep the wheels yellowed
Knowing that home is a journey
I am yet to make

While somewhere down the road
Await potential ends and destinations

Virginia's star-domed sky, cracker-box towns
And the faint whisperings of prayer
That always seem to remain

Unanswered.

The Chicago What?

Far off their tears
Buckle on the wind
While I invent rumours
Of lifeless sailboats
Sunken beneath gunmetal grey skies

Beauty surrounds me
'Tis the only excuse
I have to offer, while
Leopard-skinned waters
Gnaw at pebble and stone
In waves of childhood love-song

Such music has dumbed me
I am unable to dream of family-
Trees snapped like fishing-wire
Beneath the smoke-winged lake

I cannot see the smouldering flesh
Beached and consumed
By either fire or fire

I cannot see their cindered eyes
Dead as discovered alibis and useless
As old fingernails

I cannot find reason
In why the gospel deceived them

I am deaf to old Chicago
Walls bleeding flame - and streets

Looted and torn apart
In brutal hours of amber-whisky-red

For today
These candy-floss clouds
Could never require surgery
And rose gardens whisper
Inflammable green

Rowing boats saunter home
In the waning light of dusk

And waves chuckle - out loud -
Effortlessly rebuilding themselves

The Removal Men

They arrived
To take her out

Innocuous enough
Like detectives
On mufti day

Their thick-soled
Boots. Clopped over pave-stones
                                    Like the footfall
Of well-trained ghosts

Silhouettes of neighbours
Twitched curtains
Seeking a scent

Like unpaid hacks
Hitching a scoop
Never to be written

On the street
A small crowd had formed
In the main;

Wind-washed men
On canine patrol

Oblivious to old wives' tales
Of curiosity and cat death

While under my feet
Like dotted Lego;

School children
Homeward bound

Were told that
The men had come

Not to shift a corpse from its bed
But instead to shift a piano.

Poet Invisible on the Number 91

Hot and dry
Like the inside of a beehive
The wind claw-less
Upon brows and scalps quenched

I watch from this bird's eye rattle
The top-deck, eye-spy, unnoticed
To slip through Islington, Invisible
Traces of poetry as proof of the ghost

Stop.
Caledonian mystery
Rich eyeball the poor
Orkney house stares in dull envy
White flags hung in surrender
From ragged windowsills, thirsty for paint

Stop.
Kings Cross
Seedy bars adorned with glitter
Bow to the grand station,
An architect's perfection
Opposites attract to breathe the other skin

Stop.
Euston then Holborn
The west protects itself
Litter afraid to drop
Graffiti a mere dribble
On brickwork pristine
Homely to beggars spines

Stop.
The Strand
                    Cloaked in shadow
A thespian sightseers paradise
Ice creams drip `till slender
Cameras click like clockwork

Stop.
Trafalgar: The last stop.
Pigeons nibble the seed between my feet
I am visible once more
                    A thousand curious eyes remind me.

Dusk at Glory Farm

Season of kamikaze moths

Pollen and petals lavished
By nightfall vanishing
To become legend or prayer

Over machine-slit cornfields
Beyond the spindled oaks
There are frontiers,

Lessons to be learned
From the owlet's song of loneliness,

From Earth's sure response,
A tongue of echoes, offering
The intended mummery

In dog-eared half-light...
Darker now,

Time marches on.
Slow moans
From the black-feathered peacock
Catfights bellowing from unmapped barns

And all the while, above
Slithers of candy-floss cloud, pass
A white hammock moon,
Towards potential ends or destinations

Passages of Time

I start from the end,
Once begun
From comets' melted eyes
Only as pure as a December sun
Where all seasons entwine to forge a fifth
And the cycle of light weeps then weaves
From darkness upon darkness

We only know the corners of time
Here in the now whisper flames of old
While candlelight spills a newborn tear
And holds the dying man's last dream
Death is movement
An unseen shuffle through the stars

I start from the end
In procession
From raked bones given rise
To flee the womb of creation
Where artistry defies brushstroke
And angels awake a windless heartbeat
From silence upon silence

Yet now here
Deep in this midway forest
Where beasts tell of human skin
I wonder, is there nothing left to capture
But another ride on the merry-go-round?

We decorate all that we shall leave, even ourselves
Nest in the comfort of brickwork
Soon to be stung by change
When the clocks tread at pace

Yes, time is both footwork and firework
Our jester and hero
We are its ammunition
Its weapon and wound

And here I am
Scratching beneath each moment

Born from tomorrow's blood
                    All my knowledge merely
A slave to the imagination

I start from the end,
In succession
And forever, for me
Home is the voiceless language of the soul
Scattered in dust upon an unmarked grave.

The Dead

I think they are still in transit
Not quite ready
To leave their names
Imprinted on soil and season
Held in the breeze
Like clattering bells
Or the laughter from another house
Across the street
Voiceless, they sing
The babble in their heads
For someone, someone is still awake
Wondering of bargains or promises unmet.

Stacks

(Words Extracted From the Side of a Vinegar Bottle)

Eight generations on
And the presses remain
A day-to-day reminder

Of the long standing tradition
The unique sediment

Unpasteurised and pressed whole
Free from retention

Yet found and recognised
As old wine

Darkening in the natural haze

Bar (1am)

On trial

In a room full of Catherine-Wheel light
The air thickens and stills
Animalised and full of body heat

Late now and the club is a flurry of one-liners
Pumps spit and shut like midnight sprites
Obsessed with the aftershock of birth

Crowding my side of the bar
Four Latinos dance carefully
Aware of watchers or any waif-like
Sign of approval

Their elastic-hips sway
Like love-drunk Spanish palms
Under a glitter-licked ceiling of stars

Further in, limbs jangle
On the crowded dance-floor
Where an electric heeled few
Return to rhythms of late puberty

Back here
I serve it all up
Inaudible thoughts clanging my head,
Like broken radio

The music by this stage
Has become another blood
Encrypted in my pulse

I pour the last drink out
For a beautiful snowy faced girl

She pays and flashes a smile
That could outlast whole eras and dynasties

The till is more human
Its mouth opens like a throat

Her skin stares back at me
A hotbed of healing moss

I give her change
And watch the soda fizzle out

To become nothing.

The Witch

Her teeth were eroded tombstones in a derelict churchyard
And her hair seaweed strewn across a disused beach
And her eyes were sliced courgettes mouldy in the fridge
And her ears each an upturned question mark

Her breasts were volcanoes, dormant, once explored by Arabian travellers
And nipples were dollhouse chimneys
And her mouth was the scar on a pirate's cheekbone
And her nostrils were paper-cuts
And her tongue a lizard, dead in its skin

Her feet were those of a suffragette, chained to Parliament gates
And her knees were beehives in mid-winter
And her laugh was a Red Setter when the post drops
And her shadow was cancer in the blood

Her blood was an ashtray dunked in water
And her footprints tremors before earthquake
And her glare was trout crippled by fishhook
And her eyebrows were half-smoked strands of rolling tobacco
And her sentences were bullets in the war

Fairground

On Berryfield Green
As though it had never left,
Trace of fairground
Strong, like first scent
From the butchers knife

Once a year it came.
Fragrance of carnival
Repossessing the garden
A glittery world of elusion

Aimless noise
And undying laughter
A new world to conquer

                        Until the lick of midnight:

The House of Horrors

                        The Hall of Mirrors

The wet-greased burgers
Or the tang of candy-floss

                        Like a taste of sweet-toothed clouds

Big Wheel and Helter-skelter
Or the indelible bait of reward:
Coconut skulls to crack
Gifts for the dreamed unborn
And a clang of bells, reserved
For the strongest of men

Or the most elusive prize of all:
That girl with lilac ribbons
In her hair, Her siren-eyes,
Shimmering, swaying
As if they were composed

By the Gods themselves

Or the most likely catch of all:
A dying Goldfish,
Fin-ribbed, black-eyed
Pondering escape

In the moments it takes to forget
The wheres and whys
Of time
And space

Bethlehem

A dishevelled boy is speaking at the altar
His cinnamon skin half-lit by a lamp
His movements frail
Like an alabaster horse
Combing night-fields for figments of light

'Peace has been conjured for too long'
He says, half his face full of rage
He sits while walls choke
On the underside of his message

The church is not safe
A hotbed of blood and shrapnel

Tonight in God's house
Every hope is an errant sick-note
Every expectation shadowed by gravel-sweetness

There are only bibles to read
On the bookshelves
A young boy, crutches by his side
Approaches the end of Genesis

The older boys with guns
Decline to use them
Thinking that the church
Is some kind
Of sanctuary

Instead, they eat raw onions
Hungry, though saving bread and water
For the elderly and wounded
Too soon infected with death

Outside the boot-soles
Of oncoming soldiers
Wreath their echoes
Through the flesh of a tree

All the while, above
A great star looks down
From where it once pivoted
Now sadder than before, though
Lidless and unblinking.

101 Titles from the Chicago Institute of Contemporary Art

That which I should have done I did not do

For there is mould on the black cross
And The grand Arab (he only has sand)

Nude under a palm tree
Seated woman, spoon woman
In a red armchair
Lighting the Kerosene lamp

This, my brother is Thanksgiving
Head of a Negro woman, two gypsies
Peasant girl, equilibrium upon her shoulder

Still Life - reclining nude
Lemons on a pewter plate
Untitled woman before an aquarium

Or the eventuality of destiny
Broken and restored
Two compositions:
Portrait or invention

Or the stronghold
Birth. Title unknown
A white crucifixion

Apples at the garden
Near the lake
Birth.

Or death and life, two dancers
Tightrope walkers, life
The Dancer in Pink - and Death

The head of a soldier
The convincing reason
The triumph!
The lie.

Houses of Parliament
On stacks of wheat
Time transfixed
In water-lilies

Yet this is the turning point of the forest
Still life - certitude of the never seen
Woman standing woman
Ladies with lamps

The image disappears
Flight of the bird
At the banquet
Of air and song

And the Earth is a man
A ladder to the light
Composition or abstraction
Background with blue cloudy sky

The image disappears
Carnival - drive in the knife
Policeman manicure
Painting growth or forgotten game

In the beginning
A city landscape was untitled
In lovely blueness, purples, white and red

In the beginning
There were two philosophers
Large men of the night
Two personages in love with a woman

And memory,
Memory is a window façade
A child looking at a drawing
The formation of monsters

Memory is a woman with matches
Her visions of eternity
Or the massacre of the innocents

View from Canary Wharf

The buildings are wide-limbed, approximated
In length, almost incestuous, windows provide
An under-skin, that dances to the occasional
Rights of light

Cranes suspend in the flight path
Like amputated arms
With a flair for squad-drill

All that is definite below are skullcaps
Of moored boats, by dusk
Made real as potential gemstones

Adjoined to this, almost innocuous
A gaggle of barflies hover;
Each face exposed like a nipple
Or hysteria in the blood

At the eye's far edge
A stray bird darts westward
Along the sky
And its vast white apron

It pirouettes awhile
Pretending not to hear
The rampant fashion of human nerve

The Camdenites

Parkway, the predictable huddling of litter-dust
Of clockwork behaviour deemed strange
By those now waiting for alarms
To switch off hesitancies between dream and sleep

And what a wake-up call they are missing!
For out here love is a churchyard mannequin
Always arriving at the same skulls
Too long danced with by death

For tonight's assembled cast
Addiction has kept the mind awake
In psycho-pathetic squabbles around trashcans
To vie for nine-five discards

Out here battle-frenzy takes hold in many forms
As if the head were a violent zodiac
Governed by regimental fits
Between stillness and melancholy

Look at them bicker so late
Dead from both ends but with such energy!
Look at their great eyes, sploshed
With the light of panicked star constellations

Outside the World's End
An old man argues
With the invisible machinery of ghosts
His features dishevelled like a maimed God

The ugliness of it all diverts a slim line of traffic
Who side-step slowly, avoiding touch
For what pleasure is there
In knocking flesh half-dead?

The old man swivels sharply
Rifled by the winds upsurge

And a drop of sweat falls from his brow, one drop
That exudes a whole parable

The wind fans its tune
On the ashen-faced walls
Where a young girl is junked out
Sprawled like rare wet limestone

Look at her snowy face
Decorated by sound, look!
Her skin speaks volumes
Of how pain never quite teaches us enough

Nailing

Eyes coal-heavy, I woke
To the sound of an upstairs tenant
Nailing some girl through the floorboards

I was not sure
How long they had been at it

But their rhythm suggested
A climactic period -

Her dizzy raptures
His home-stretch tremor of static

Knowing my neighbours
Only by face
I wondered
Which one of them it was
Up there

My mind revolved
Choicelessly corrupted

I was forced
To picture every male face
In the entire building
Pasted with that animalised
Orgasm-point expression

Not done yet, indisputably irrespectable
I strayed further afield
And imagined the woman -
Who was she?

After all,
There had been no bed-squeaking before
She could look like anyone

In minutes I imagined
Every combination
Of woman possible

By which time (for them at least)
It was all over,
Just low hushed tones
And the faint striking of a match

Hurriedly, dressing
I realised how exhausted I felt

Stepping outside,
Into the silent antiseptic air.

Spitting Images

I keep seeing myself
In the white of the moon
At midnight

Or in that field
As the old man
Tending a fire
By the hedge
Trying to extinguish
Flames of age

On streets, back-alleys
At the fruit stand on Waterloo
Fingering peaches
Seeking out ripeness

Me I tell you
Same age
Same face,
Same clenched fist

Just now
There I was
In the flux and flow
Of the crowd

I was that
Approaching stranger

Until I turned
Into someone else.

Touch or Absence

'If when alone at times
I were to describe
How a solitary white dove
Harbours in your heart
Flying to a far skies calling
How your patience is earth old
And your touch celestial
How you sing to me
On nights like this
Like a river lost in thought
How when we touch
We decorate every silence'

Bindings

(For Mark Williams)

Was it the way we named birdsong in the shapeless fog
That bound us? Or the way we made our own tone
To the phrase 'hopelessly lost'
On seeing the countryside drunk,
His face mushroomed into acres of pain

How it stamped some common ground
Adding vowel-texture to the dogs erratic barking
Or the in-between sounds of a pepper-mill being scrunched
While your mother hovered over pans,
And loosened the blurred mesh of cutlery from a drawer

Remember how we walked the coast
Of a leopard-skinned sea
To look for hidden origins of rain
How those distant rock formations appeared to us
Angel-headed in the distance

As if they were carved
From soot and shadow.
And how those two fishing boats
Named 'Tranquillity' and 'Freedom'
Spoke to us in the only language they knew.

Lament of Adam

Last night I returned to Eden
And blamed the morning dew

Last night I returned to Eden
And caught a wisp of enticement
In the knuckled oaks
Where Aeolus once fled
In a summer of Pythons

My dreamed love and I
We were the first
To picnic that garden
Unknowing of immoral fruits

We were simple folk. Snug
In love's jewelled skin
In a quest for geometric antiquity
We were carved
Like gargoyles and hymns
Across a blackboard of infinity

To us, motive was the possible blood
Of our unborn children
To us, clarity had not learnt to chew bone
And the great puppeteer appeared
In a tapestry of dreams

I realise it now,
Why the passerines appeared concerned

But back then
I presumed laughter or coded sonnets (Ignorant to my size)
I thought the wooden hiss was confirmation
Of tomorrow's green rose

Easy to cleanse the scars of a broken world
When drunk on hindsight

Back then we trusted all we knew
And all we knew was this
Impossible song of flesh

And being life's latest symphony
We knew nothing of death
Nothing of darkness,
Humming in the tree

So we made our one witless presumption
That truth could bind with beauty.

Everything Must Die (but the seed)

Her voice was all the places
I yearned to travel - only human

Yet now - hearing it
Is like fishbone in my throat

Stuck. I have never felt
So many unlit matches inside me.

These are the days of forfeit
Fists banging rosaries

These are the days of knowing
Everything must die but the seed.

All the words - the feckless catcalls
I used in absence to describe

How she turned from my light
For the very last time
Dark now.
I summon the half-wit jester
Stored or hung in my head

Who witlessly declares;
'Such defiance will set you free'

Foolish milksop!
For tonight each shadow is painted
Blacker than before
And cars hum on by like mad old drunks

Silhouettes of couples kiss
As if to remind me;

Everything must die
But the seed.

The Potential Asylum of a Moment

Behind me
The world was a strange place

I spoke in wishbone
And angels contended:
'You have seen enough
of love'

And time -
Time was ablaze
A tremor of clocks

Serpent or saviour
Depending
On your picture
Of the flame

And while each teardrop poured
So sweetly
On the cusp
Of a broken glass

And I kept thinking
Of nothings and scars
Yet meaning you.

Playgrounds to inhabit
Half-reaching
For touch
Or loss

Depending on your point of view.

Flowers

I remember the girl
who used to pass me
flowers through the gap
in our wooden fence

I see her still, oftentimes
eyeing the boy I was
her beauty a bruise, pristine
and her face
as if composed
by the angels themselves

strange how
her name escapes me

but I think she knew
back then, a sense
of the sublime,
the unknowing
significance of touch

I wonder what she does now
what paths, what envelopes
she might have opened…

A florist perhaps
where she still passes
from garden to garden?

and I wonder
if those flowers
she once sent me
through the gap
in our wooden fence
will ever learn how to grow.

Grandma's House

She lived here many moons ago
It was all different back then

The tenth step of the stairway never creaked
The gap between the bathroom and ceiling window never leaked

But that's changed now
Towels are disordered hanging from hooks
Scattered magazines have replaced dust-ridden books
Odours of peppermint tea have been replaced
By the stale stench of Amber Leaf

The bronze pot where nightly she soaked
Her false teeth, is now an ashtray
Cluttered with butts
Burning away her memory.

Art

A passing breath of flesh I was
Like the life of footprints among sand
Transience among the dead I was
Artistry in the palm of her hand

The Lucy Poem

My love for you is the feather
Embedded in a wasteland of tongues
A faint whisper of snowfall
                    Between song and permanence

My love for you resides
In white toothless want,
Deferred laughter, echoing
In children's playgrounds
When schooldays are done

My love for you is the intended poem
I long to write, on the canvas of sunset
A picture I am yet to paint, from memory

Of gulls suspended at the oceans edge
Silhouettes adrift, in pools of salted scarlet

My love for you is the poppy seed's
Impression of red

The garden dream I have
Night after night, reoccurring

My love for you is the moment I wake
To a scent of jasmine and Birchwood
Knowing the garden grows on without me.

Allergies of Ice

Your ice had breath
Ask each stony hunch in this city
Never once did I imagine metals to spasm
From customary effects of wind-wound

So cold!
Ask the roses
They have enough mouths
For some filament of truth to out

I have walked the garden myself
Done your rounds, snagged my teeth
On archived apertures of autumn

What furies and memories these are
Impossible to bind!

For a brief while
You worked on me
Nightshift, overtime

Accentual in my sleep-patterns
And though I was tongued the dreamer
I felt stationed like an eye-witness
Sibling offered morning advice:
'Brother, in all darkness there is a face'

How true and so often hidden
Like a faded teardrop
In the preface of an old book

In all darkness there is a face
Your face, soft as water, with whispers
That turn into killings.

For days on end
I tried not to listen
But slowly the sounds crept into my ears
Like a legion of kamikaze wasps

Dumb creature I was, rammed with allergy
I knew little of how to survive
Having never once been stung before.

Mannequin

You are mannequin

Beautiful, cold and merciless,
Squeezing blood from the broken
Bell of my sleep. Your peacock feathers
Shoelace my abdomen in some
Blue-vein, new-wave fashion

And granted, I ask for it this way
By sucking on the stale draughts
Of air you leave behind
Placing my burning wants
Into your crippled shades of black

You call me back at strange hours
Udder heavy with silences
That crack over me like eggs,
Hooking me in, a fat trout
By the root of my tongue

I stumble through you, like a war.
In your flowerbed,
Wishing that I was a god
So I could invent you
A better world in seven days

Yet I would always crave
Another hour to hear if your heart
Could form inside my skin
Where we would become one echo
Singing forever on the waterish ice.

Strange Length of the Word Goodbye

We both know it is the end of the road
Yet my smoke-rings would swirl
Into perfect hearts for you

In an hour…

Less now

I will be walking in the rain
Over Westminster Bridge
And every drop will be you

Saying your goodbyes
Staining my thumbnails
For the very last time.

While You Sleep

You must be near the 39th wink
Slipped from the claws of a whisky dose
Chasing miracles through forest dreams

I look at London, dry
Long since crawled from the bunk
Over a sleepy Thames you stir,
Mesmeric.

Westminster reminds me
Of your carved elegance
Today I will see you in all places
Etched upon my mind
From billboards of Piccadilly
To Soho dingy backstreets

Like a tired knuckle, you uncurl
Into the palm of morning
To jigsaw pieces beyond the blanket
The riddle of consequence

I skip back to a midnight laced with magic
A warm caress before the cobweb of dawn
When eyelids were hypnotised of time

You stare through branches and rooftops
And mop up the evidence
Droplets of wine on oak
Leftovers of a salad drowned

I see a smile flicker in your lips
And cradle the hours we had
Spent free.

Amnesty

(for M.)

By the time I told you
What I wanted to say
Some twenty years had passed
And I was not sure if I meant it anymore

All that time
Bled like blossom
Snagged on a bed of ferns

All that time
With too much to say
About the victory of ignorance
Inside us both

I feared every nerve-terminal
And all those un-enduring realities
Of time

Days passed, looped together
Became weeks and eras

By the time I told you
What I wanted to say
Some twenty years of fermented love
Had filled the nucleus of my heart
And I was not sure if I meant it anymore

Tonight I count each star
From the eclipse of my window
And imagine our silences
Breathing through the cherry trees.

Footprints in the Sand

Your footprints may be long gone, washed up
Even your feet may not remember anything
Yet never forget that lonely stretch of sand you walked
Before the night grew velvet and stars budded into globes of white wax
Never forget how the coast sucks and spits the entire weight of a tidal pulse
Curling like an infinite honey-rust vine through dusk-shimmer and beyond

Your footprints may be long gone
Salt-smudge on your lips buried deep like a garden bone
Yet the whole earth palpitates even through its silences
As if it were a dead man whose nightly cries fire from the grave.
Never forget that smile you gave as the wind washed each pore of your face
With breath like an angel sighing at birdsong flung from granite-grey skies
And with eyes quarried from indecipherable intimacies between soil and skin

Never forget that lonely stretch of sand you walked for hours on end
Staring through hymnal horizons to a sea with its endless ribs and elegies
Never forget the dappled fish singing chamber music from streams,
The musty language of seaweed, the far-off rock so immovable
As if it were home to all echo and location

Though memory will never be the moment it truly desires
Though our hands may grow fabled with age,
And our minds become uncertain of the heart's intended song
Never forget that lonely stretch of sand you walked for hours on end
It remembers you now and your footprints when they are gone.

Forestry

Because what I believe in is fiction
Or a hazard to others
Summer rains quickening
In the pulse of a cloud
The terror and infinity
Immersed in a single grain of sand
Or the mysterious now of your breath
Attuned to the in-betweens of an old oak tree
Because such things speak to me
Like blood in a coral
Often I must walk alone
Laconic and sorrowing

The Tunnel Synopsis

'Life without music would be a mistake'
(F.Neitzche)

This is all I remember:
There were mistakes and tunnels
And some moments in-between
Where rhythm was just a distant arc of gravity
After low-hushed cantillations of rain
The sun would suddenly flare up
But I would hear nothing
But silence without volume
I don't know if the light was military
Or just a space that love couldn't occupy
I thought the Spanish castanets signified
Old boy-cries of 'Wolf'
This is all I remember:
Though no doubt there were other nights
Or other faces I avoided.